Our Values

ACTIVISM & VOLUNTEERING

by

John Wood

CRABTREE
PUBLISHING COMPANY
WWW.CRABTREEBOOKS.COM

CRABTREE PUBLISHING COMPANY
WWW.CRABTREEBOOKS.COM

**Published
in Canada
Crabtree Publishing**
616 Welland Avenue
St. Catharines, ON
L2M 5V6

**Published in
the United States
Crabtree Publishing**
PMB 59051
350 Fifth Ave, 59th Floor
New York, NY 10118

Published in 2019 by Crabtree Publishing Company

First Published by Book Life in 2018
Copyright © 2018 Book Life

Author: John Wood

Editors: Holly Duhig, Janine Deschenes

Design: Danielle Rippengill

Proofreader: Melissa Boyce

Print and production coordinator:
  Katherine Berti

All facts, statistics, web addresses and URLs in this book were verified as valid and accurate at time of writing. No responsibility for any changes to external websites or references can be accepted by either the author or publisher.

Printed in the U.S.A./122018/CG20181005

Photographs
Shutterstock
  1000 Words: p. 9
    (center left)
  a katz: p. 21 (top)
  Alessandro Pietri: p. 13
    (bottom right)
  Anita van den Broek:
    front cover (bottom)
  Avivi Aharon: p. 8 (top)
  BAKOUNINE: p. 23
    (bottom left)
  chrisdorney: p. 11 (bottom)
  CL Shebley: p. 11 (top)
  fitzcrittle: p. 6 (center)
  Fotos593: p. 13 (top left)
  Hung Chung Chih: p. 12
    (bottom left)
  Kim Wilson: p. 17 (bottom)
  Mihai Speteanu: p. 2
  MinhHue: p. 4 (bottom)
  Saikat Paul: p. 16
    (bottom left)
  Vergani Fotografia: p. 21
    (bottom)
  Worawee Meepian: p. 24
    (center right)
Wikimedia Commons
  AgnosticPreachersKid:
    p. 22 (center left)
  Centers for Disease
Control and Prevention:
    p. 18 (center right)
First Lady of the United
States Twitter account:
    p. 9 (bottom right)
FotoDuets, Kennet1:
    p. 24 (center left)
LSE Library: p. 18
    (center right)
NASA: p. 19 (top left)
National Institute for
Occupational Safety and
    Health (NIOSH): p. 12
    (center right)
Pete Souza: p. 10 (bottom)
Pierre–Selim: p. 22
    (bottom left), 23
    (top left)
R. M. Calamar: p. 10
    (center left)
The All–Nite Images from
    NY, NY, USA: p. 15
    (bottom)
U.S. Marine Corps: p. 19
    (bottom)
uwdigitalcollections:
    p. 14 (bottom right)
Worawee Meepian:
    p. 25 (center left)
All other images by
  Shutterstock

Library and Archives Canada Cataloguing in Publication

Wood, John, 1990-, author
    Activism and volunteering / John Wood.

(Our values)
Includes index.
Issued in print and electronic formats.
ISBN 978-0-7787-5436-7 (hardcover).--
ISBN 978-0-7787-5499-2 (softcover).--
ISBN 978-1-4271-2227-8 (HTML)

    1. Social action--Juvenile literature. 2. Voluntarism--Juvenile literature. 3. Social movements--Juvenile literature. 4. Volunteers--Juvenile literature. 5. Reformers--Juvenile literature. I. Title.

HN18.3.W567 2018   j361.2   C2018-905505-7
                                                            C2018-905506-5

Library of Congress Cataloging-in-Publication Data

Names: Wood, John, author.
Title: Activism and volunteering / John Wood.
Description: New York : Crabtree Publishing Company, [2018] |
  Series: Our values | Includes index.
Identifiers: LCCN 2018043794 (print) | LCCN 2018045853 (ebook) |
  ISBN 9781427122278 (Electronic) |
  ISBN 9780778754367 (hardcover) |
  ISBN 9780778754992 (pbk.)
Subjects: LCSH: Voluntarism--Juvenile literature. | Volunteers--Juvenile
  literature. | Social action--Juvenile literature. | Political
  participation--Juvenile literature.
Classification: LCC HN49.V64 (ebook) | LCC HN49.V64 D84 2018 (print) |
  DDC 302/.14--dc23
LC record available at https://lccn.loc.gov/2018043794

CONTENTS

Words that are **boldfaced** can be found in the glossary on page 31.

WHAT IS VOLUNTEERING?

Most people spend their days going to work, going to school, taking care of their homes, and doing the activities outside of school and work that make them happy. One activity that many people find rewarding is volunteering. To volunteer is to spend time and effort doing something, without receiving something in return. Usually, volunteering refers to offering time or effort to help a cause, such as making sure that everyone's needs are met in a community. Volunteering might also be done to help fix a problem in a community, such as a lack of trees.

A PERSON WHO TAKES PART IN VOLUNTEERING IS CALLED A VOLUNTEER.

VOLUNTEERS ARE NEEDED TO HOST EVENTS LIKE THIS CHARITY RUN IN VIETNAM.

Volunteers do not get anything in return for their work. However, the work that they do is very important because it helps people in need. A person might volunteer because they care about a particular cause. They might feel that volunteering helps them to make a difference or to give back to their community. Helping other people and working to fix problems can also make a volunteer feel rewarded.

CHARITIES AND NONPROFITS

Volunteers often work for charities or nonprofit organizations. A charity or charitable organization is an organization that supports and raises money for a charitable cause. A charitable cause is usually known as something that assists people in need. Charities might work to provide education for students who cannot afford to go to school, or collect food to feed hungry community members. Charities are nonprofit organizations. This means that the profit, or money, that they make goes into supporting the cause, instead of going into paying employees or owners, as a regular business might operate. All charities are nonprofit organizations, but not all nonprofit organizations are charities. A nonprofit organization that is not a charity might support a noncharitable cause, such as creating sports programs for youth in a community. Nonprofits still support a good cause that benefits people in a community, but if their cause is not considered charitable, they are not considered charities. Usually, a country's government decides if an organization is a charity or a nonprofit. The government might provide money to pay the people who run the charity or nonprofit.

A 2015 SURVEY SHOWED THAT ABOUT 25 PERCENT OF AMERICANS VOLUNTEERED THAT YEAR. A CANADIAN SURVEY SHOWED THAT 44 PERCENT OF PEOPLE VOLUNTEERED IN 2013.

WAYS OF VOLUNTEERING

Many charities and nonprofits recruit and organize volunteers to work for their cause. This means it is possible for them to spend all of the money they raise on the cause—rather than paying workers. Some volunteers work together in a big group to organize a large charity event or project. Some volunteers might help with day-to-day activities of a charity, such as cooking in a soup kitchen. Other volunteers work alone. An individual volunteer might visit a senior citizen or a person with disabilities, to help care for them and give them company.

TYPES OF VOLUNTEERING

EVENTS

Most events are paid for by selling tickets. For example, people pay money to go to a concert or sports event. The money made from tickets pays for the performers, the workers who run the event, and any other costs. Charity events are a little different. They need to make as much money as possible to help a cause. The cost of the event has to be much less than the money they make. This makes it difficult to pay someone to keep the event running. Many people volunteer to run the event and help out any way they can, so that the charity can spend all of the money raised at an event on the cause itself.

THE AMERICAN CANCER SOCIETY ORGANIZES EVENTS SUCH AS "MAKING STRIDES AGAINST BREAST CANCER." THESE EVENTS, HELD IN CITIES ACROSS THE COUNTRY, ARE WALKS THAT RAISE MONEY FOR BREAST CANCER RESEARCH AND PREVENTION.

CREATING AND DONATING

Some volunteers give their time to create and donate things that will help others. For example, people might knit warm clothes and teddy bears and send them to a charity, which will then give them to babies and toddlers. A volunteer might teach a class on dancing, painting, or music to youth or adults who could not otherwise afford such classes. Other volunteers might bake desserts, which can be sold by charities to raise money for a good cause.

CHARITIES WILL OFTEN HELP MATCH VOLUNTEERS TO THE PEOPLE THEY WILL VISIT.

SPENDING TIME WITH OTHERS

Some people live alone and find it hard to go outside and meet other people. This might be because they have an illness or a disability, or because they are elderly and find it difficult to move around. Many senior citizens live alone, and may not have anyone to talk to. Studies have shown that loneliness is a big problem for people as they age. It even negatively affects their health. Some volunteers visit lonely people and spend time with them. People also volunteer by visiting people in hospitals.

SMALL TASKS AND JOBS

Many volunteers give up their time to do small tasks or jobs for one person, or for their community. For example, a group of volunteers might paint the walls of a hospital or pick up trash in a park. Other volunteers might bring groceries to senior citizens, or help someone who is disabled with jobs around the house. This kind of volunteering makes their community a better place. It is sometimes organized by a charity or nonprofit, but people can volunteer to do small jobs on their own, too.

PROGRAMS THAT MAKE A DIFFERENCE

Some volunteers work with an organization to run programs that make a difference in the lives of people in need. They might help a charity run a store in which people can buy clothing or other goods at discounted prices. They might help run a support group for children who have experienced loss, or for survivors of traumatic experiences. They are a big part of making a difference in their communities.

THESE VOLUNTEERS ARE CLEANING UP A PARK TOGETHER.

WHAT IS ACTIVISM?

Activism is a way of **campaigning** or **actively** calling for change. It is commonly used to bring about political or social change. Political change refers to changes in the way countries, states and provinces, and communities are run by governments. It sometimes refers to change in the people who are part of government. Social changes are differences in the way society thinks and behaves. It might involve **persuading** other people to change how they feel about certain issues, or convincing others to change their behavior. Many activists are also volunteers because they give up their time to spread ideas and information about an issue. Activism can also be a part of someone's work or day-to-day activities.

THERE IS NO PLANET B

A PERSON WHO CARRIES OUT ACTIVISM IS CALLED AN ACTIVIST.

CHANGING THE WORLD

People don't always agree about certain issues, such as what the laws of a country should be, or how important it is to save the environment. An activist wants to change people's opinions. Activism can start off as a small action. For example, activists may **protest** in front of a clothing store if they believe that the company uses **child labor** to make their clothes. They might tell customers about the practice as they enter a store. Or, an activist might speak out against the high use of plastic because of the damage it does to the environment. They might try to convince others to use reusable goods instead of discarding plastic ones. If enough people protest against an issue, they might bring about change.

ACTIVISM CAN INCLUDE SPREADING A MESSAGE, OR INFORMING PEOPLE ABOUT AN ISSUE.

SPEAKING UP

Activism is important because it often gives a voice to causes and people who might be unable to speak for themselves. Animals who are hurt by humans aren't able to speak up for themselves. Workers being mistreated might be unable to protest because they fear losing their jobs. **Unethical** companies and governments might also ignore or cover up issues. They might purposely silence anyone who disagrees with them. For example, the American science and engineering company DuPont deliberately hid evidence that a **chemical** they used was poisoning workers and community members who lived near their factory in West Virginia. Activism is a way of bringing attention to a topic that might be hidden. This makes activism an extremely important step in dealing with issues around the world.

MICHELLE OBAMA USED THE MESSAGE #BRINGBACKOURGIRLS ON TWITTER TO BRING ATTENTION TO THE KIDNAPPING OF HUNDREDS OF SCHOOLGIRLS IN NIGERIA. HER MESSAGE IS AN EXAMPLE OF ACTIVISM THAT TRIES TO GIVE A VOICE TO PEOPLE WHO ARE UNABLE TO SPEAK OUT FOR THEMSELVES.

Activists come from all sorts of backgrounds. Although activists who support a certain cause may live all over the world, they are all linked by their common goal: to make change. Communication is important to keep activists together, and to organize projects, marches, and protests. The Internet has made activism much more powerful. It is now easier for those who feel strongly about an issue to find each other, and to work together.

TYPES OF ACTIVISM

BOYCOTTING

Some activists deliberately choose not to use or buy certain things as a type of protest. This is called boycotting. An activist might boycott products made by a company they believe is unethical. Activists might also boycott products which are bad for the environment or that harm animals. Services, such as airlines or electricity companies, can also be boycotted. Sometimes, activists boycott travel to certain countries to protest issues that happen there, or to show that they disagree with a country's leader or government.

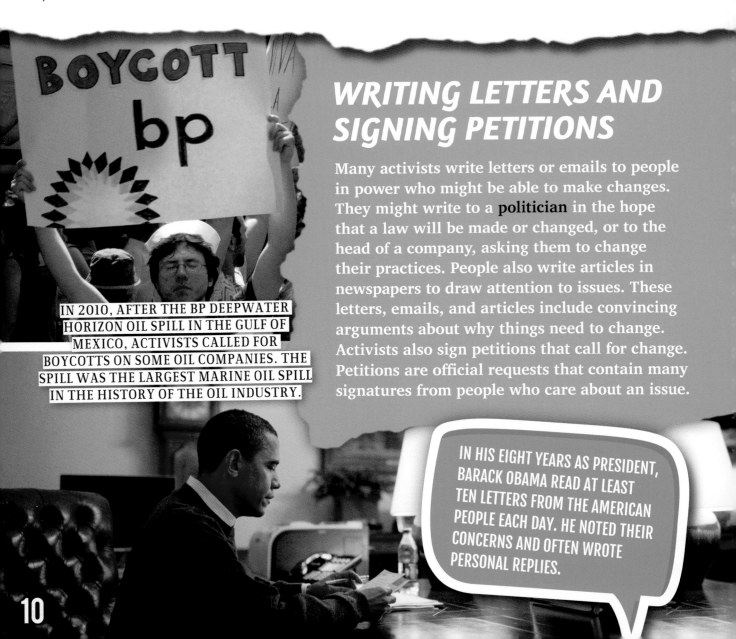

IN 2010, AFTER THE BP DEEPWATER HORIZON OIL SPILL IN THE GULF OF MEXICO, ACTIVISTS CALLED FOR BOYCOTTS ON SOME OIL COMPANIES. THE SPILL WAS THE LARGEST MARINE OIL SPILL IN THE HISTORY OF THE OIL INDUSTRY.

WRITING LETTERS AND SIGNING PETITIONS

Many activists write letters or emails to people in power who might be able to make changes. They might write to a **politician** in the hope that a law will be made or changed, or to the head of a company, asking them to change their practices. People also write articles in newspapers to draw attention to issues. These letters, emails, and articles include convincing arguments about why things need to change. Activists also sign petitions that call for change. Petitions are official requests that contain many signatures from people who care about an issue.

IN HIS EIGHT YEARS AS PRESIDENT, BARACK OBAMA READ AT LEAST TEN LETTERS FROM THE AMERICAN PEOPLE EACH DAY. HE NOTED THEIR CONCERNS AND OFTEN WROTE PERSONAL REPLIES.

MARCHES, PROTESTS, AND DEMONSTRATIONS

Protests are events in which activists gather together to speak out about an issue and call for change. A march is a type of protest during which a group of activists walk in a **procession** in a public place. A demonstration is a protest, too. It is usually a public meeting that may or may not involve marching. At protests, people might hold signs and chant words that represent their point of view. People might also organize

a **sit-in**, refusing to leave a place until their voices are heard or demands are met. Usually, the more people who come to a protest, the more **media coverage** the cause receives. Media coverage can help to get the message out to even more people. Most protests are peaceful. Peaceful protests are important because violence hurts people and often distracts others from the issues being discussed.

ART

Many pieces of great art have been created as a form of activism. For example, songs might use lyrics to tell people about a cause and why it is important. Public **art installations** and **graffiti** can draw attention to such things as environmental issues and cases of **injustice** around the world. Popular art can reach a lot of people, so it is a good way of spreading information and bringing about change.

BANKSY IS A FAMOUS GRAFFITI ARTIST WHOSE WORK OFTEN DRAWS ATTENTION TO ISSUES. ALTHOUGH HIS MOTIVATIONS ARE OFTEN UNKNOWN, THIS PIECE IN LONDON, ENGLAND IS THOUGHT TO BE A STATEMENT AGAINST **GOVERNMENT SURVEILLANCE** OF CITIZENS.

COMMON CAUSES FOR
VOLUNTEERING AND ACTIVISM

THE ENVIRONMENT

The environment on Earth has been damaged by human activity. **Carbon dioxide** emitted from cars, airplanes, and power plants is trapping heat in Earth's atmosphere, causing **global warming**.

Plastic and garbage is filling the oceans and killing the animals and fish which live there. Deforestation and large-scale farming destroys the habitats of plants and animals all over the world.

To help the environment, volunteers might pick up and recycle trash and litter. Cleanups might be organized in such places as parks and beaches. Volunteers might also work for charities and nonprofits such as Greenpeace, which supports environmental conservation and protection around the world. Greenpeace also promotes activism to help protect the environment. Environmental activists might organize protests to draw attention to an environmental issue, sign petitions to persuade governments to cut carbon emissions, or boycott products that are damaging to the environment.

VOLUNTEERS WORKED HARD TO CLEAN UP AFFECTED BEACHES AFTER THE DEEPWATER HORIZON OIL SPILL IN 2010.

In recent years, thousands of Chinese activists have protested for cleaner air. Air pollution is a big issue in China's major cities. In some places, gas masks were put on statues to send a message about the dangerous air pollution. They hope the Chinese government will listen to their concerns and make changes to improve the health of people and the environment.

IN BEIJING, MANY PEOPLE WEAR MASKS TO AVOID BREATHING IN POLLUTED AIR.

LARGE CROWDS OF PEOPLE GATHERED TO HAND OUT SUPPLIES TO SURVIVORS OF AN EARTHQUAKE IN QUITO, ECUADOR IN 2016.

DISEASES AND DISASTERS

Many volunteers and activists work to raise awareness, money, or other kinds of help for people affected by diseases and disasters. Often, money needs to be raised to pay for research into disease treatment and prevention. For many diseases, research is being done to find cures. Money and awareness are also raised for people who suffer from diseases, but do not have access to health care or treatment.

After a natural disaster, such as a hurricane or earthquake, there is often a volunteer effort to help those affected. Volunteers might travel to the place where the disaster happened to hand out food, water, and blankets, or help reconstruct buildings that have been damaged or destroyed. Doctors might volunteer their services to help people who are ill or injured in a disaster. Volunteers might also organize efforts at home, such as clothing or food **drives**, to gather money and supplies to send to those in need.

Activism can shine a light on those who need help and health care. Activists might also criticize or speak out against an organization or government's treatment of a disaster. For example, some activists in the United States have protested against the U.S. government's treatment of the relief effort for Hurricane Maria victims in Puerto Rico. They feel the government did not do enough to help survivors.

IN AUGUST 2018, THE GOVERNMENT OF PUERTO RICO ESTIMATED THAT ALMOST 3,000 PEOPLE DIED DURING AND AFTER HURRICANE MARIA.

POLITICS AND WAR

In most **democratic** countries, governments hold elections every few years. An election is a vote which decides which politicians will be in charge of the country. Most adults in a country try to affect political change by voting. It's one way that people can be an active part of political change. Other people, however, go further than voting by volunteering for political causes or **parties**, or by taking part in activism to speak about political issues.

Volunteers often give their time to help support political parties. Usually, most of the volunteering happens before an election, because volunteers hope to gather votes for the party they support. A volunteer for a political party might hand out information about the party's ideas and plans if they are elected into government. Activists might work to change people's minds about certain political parties and issues, or speak out about government decisions with which they disagree. In Ontario, Canada, in 2018, teen students organized a walkout to protest the newly elected provincial government's decision to stop teaching the updated sexual education curriculum. They used the hashtag #Wethestudentsdonotconsent to speak out against their government's change.

Wars are sometimes outcomes of political changes. When leaders change, they may cause conflict in their country or with other countries. If a country is at war, **refugees** might flee the country for safety. Volunteers might raise money and supplies for refugees or help set up refugee camps, which look after these people and provide them with food and shelter. Activism is a way to speak out against war. In the 1960s, American activists called for an end to the Vietnam War. The activism had a big impact on how the war was perceived, or seen, by Americans.

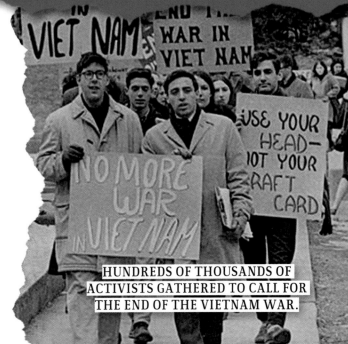

HUNDREDS OF THOUSANDS OF ACTIVISTS GATHERED TO CALL FOR THE END OF THE VIETNAM WAR.

INEQUALITY

Not everybody is treated equally, or has the same opportunities in life. Some people face **discrimination**, **racism**, or other inequality because of their gender, their religion, or their race. A difference in how people are treated is called inequality. Combating inequality in communities, countries, and the world is a common reason why people volunteer or take part in activism.

Volunteers might try to fight inequality by helping people who have less than others. Volunteers might work in soup kitchens and give out food to homeless people. They could build and repair buildings in the community. There are also volunteers who offer free extracurricular activities or offer lessons to people who could not otherwise afford them.

THESE VOLUNTEERS ARE SERVING FOOD TO PEOPLE WHO NEED HELP MEETING SOME OF THEIR BASIC NEEDS.

Activism is one of the most important ways to fight inequality. It is one way that people can speak out about injustice. Protests and letters to politicians can show people that something is unfair, and that things need to change. Speaking out about one's own experiences of inequality can also be a form of activism. The Black Lives Matter movement (above) stages protests to draw attention to the inequality in the way black Americans are treated by the police. Activists speak out about police brutality and other violence targeted at black citizens.

WHY DO PEOPLE GET INVOLVED?

CONTRIBUTING TO THE GOOD

Volunteers and activists might support a cause or work to help others because they believe that all people deserve equal opportunities. Some people feel as though the world is a good place, which has helped them and provided them with positive opportunities. They volunteer or become activists because they feel they should give something back to the world. They believe that everyone who is able should help others in our global community. Volunteering and activism are a way of doing something good for the world.

AT SCHOOL, STUDENTS MIGHT CONTRIBUTE TO A POSITIVE SCHOOL COMMUNITY BY VOLUNTEERING TO TUTOR OTHER STUDENTS.

FIGHTING AGAINST THE BAD

Many volunteers and activists think that there is too much injustice in the world. They might feel it is important that someone stands up for those who are experiencing such things, and who may not be able to speak up for themselves. Volunteering and activism is one way to fight against injustice. It can also make people feel like they can make a positive difference in the global community.

"INJUSTICE ANYWHERE IS A THREAT TO JUSTICE EVERYWHERE"

THIS MAN IN INDIA IS SPEAKING UP FOR HUMAN RIGHTS AROUND THE WORLD.

PEOPLE WHO LIKE ANIMALS CAN SHARE THAT PASSION WITH OTHERS BY VOLUNTEERING IN AN ANIMAL SHELTER.

FOLLOWING PASSIONS

Volunteering and activism can be a way for people to get involved in something about which they are passionate. To be passionate means to have strong feelings about something. Getting involved is a way that people can learn more about their passions and feel rewarded in the activities they pursue. Volunteering and activism can also be a great way to meet new people, to share our passions with others, and to learn about others' passions. By getting involved in volunteering and activism, people can understand new things, and begin to look at the world in completely new and different ways.

Getting involved in volunteering and activism may seem like a small way of helping big issues. However, if every person makes a small difference where they live, the whole world improves. One person cannot change the world alone, but a real difference can be made when people work together.

A SINGLE ACT OF ACTIVISM MAY SEEM SMALL. BUT WHEN MANY ACTIVISTS GET TOGETHER, SUCH AS THE PEOPLE AT THIS SAN FRANCISCO DEMONSTRATION IN SUPPORT OF HEALTH CARE, CHANGE CAN BE ACHIEVED.

ACHIEVEMENTS OF VOLUNTEERING AND ACTIVISM

The dedicated work of activists and volunteers have brought about important changes throughout history. Here are some of them.

EMMELINE PANKHURST

EMMELINE PANKHURST AND WOMEN'S SUFFRAGE

Emmeline Pankhurst was a British political activist who campaigned for women's suffrage, or the right to vote, in the late 1800s and early 1900s. She and other women fought for the right to vote by organizing demonstrations and going on hunger strikes. As a result, in 1918, some women over the age of 30 were given the right to vote. Pankhurst is an important figure in women's suffrage worldwide. In the United States, women such as Susan B. Anthony and Elizabeth Cady Stanton helped win the right to vote in 1920. Canadian activists Mary Ann Shadd and Dr. Emily Howard Stowe helped secure women's suffrage in 1918—though Asian and **Indigenous** women did not receive the right until decades later.

THE WORK OF PANKHURST AND OTHER WOMEN WAS A BIG PART OF WOMEN WINNING THE RIGHT TO VOTE. SHE EVEN TRAVELED TO THE UNITED STATES TO SPEAK ABOUT THE ISSUE.

THE EBOLA OUTBREAK

In 2014, a disease called Ebola spread across West African countries such as Sierra Leone, Liberia, and Guinea. Thousands of people died. In response, charities, doctors, and volunteers all over the world sent help to provide health care, and stop the disease from spreading further. The World Health Organization (WHO) has said these countries are, for now, Ebola free. Without the help of volunteers, this wouldn't be possible.

THIS MAP SHOWS THE AREAS MOST AFFECTED BY THE OUTBREAK.

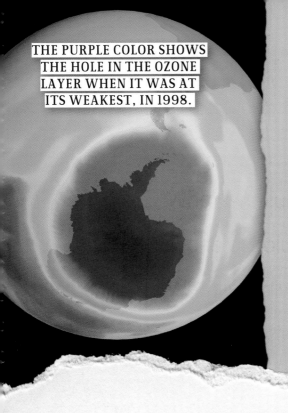

THE PURPLE COLOR SHOWS THE HOLE IN THE OZONE LAYER WHEN IT WAS AT ITS WEAKEST, IN 1998.

THE MONTRÉAL PROTOCOL

Environmental activism gained more support in the 1900s. Scientists and activists drew attention to the negative impact humans were having on the planet, and world leaders realized that something needed to be done. This led to a very important agreement in 1987, called the Montréal Protocol on **Substances** that Deplete the Ozone Layer. Many countries signed the agreement, pledging to stop making and using substances that destroyed Earth's **ozone layer**. While there is still much to be done in the fight against **climate change**, the hole in the ozone layer is now shrinking, which is a success that came from the Montréal Protocol.

DR. MARTIN LUTHER KING JR.

Dr. Martin Luther King Jr. was an activist who campaigned for equality for African Americans. He was a leader of the civil rights movement, which protested racial **segregation** and discrimination in the United States. Dr. King and his followers took part in peaceful protests and sit-ins. He is most famous for his "I Have a Dream" speech, in which he talks about a future where black people and white people live together equally and have equal opportunities. Dr. King inspired many people to join the civil rights movement. In 1964, the U.S. Civil Rights Act outlawed discrimination and segregation based on race, gender, religion, and other characteristics.

DR. MARTIN LUTHER KING JR. WAS AWARDED THE NOBEL PEACE PRIZE IN 1964. HE WAS KILLED IN 1968.

BUILDING COMMUNITIES

WHAT IS A COMMUNITY?

A community is a group of people who live, work, and play in a place. Any group can be a community. Communities might be all of the students and staff at a school, or the people who live in a small town. Communities can be large cities, too. They can even be countries. We are all part of a global community too. This is the idea that everyone who lives on Earth is connected as part of one community. Belonging to a community is important because people in communities help each other and work together. By getting involved in volunteering and activism, you can positively impact all of the communities of which you are part.

WHAT COMMUNITIES ARE YOU PART OF? HOW DOES VOLUNTEERING AND ACTIVISM IMPROVE THEM?

Sometimes people feel disconnected from their communities. They may believe that they don't have anything in common with others around them or that they aren't important parts of their community. They might feel that they can't make a difference or improve the lives of others in their communities. Volunteering and activism is a good way to fight feelings of disconnect within a community. They build stronger communities and bring people together to work for common causes. They are an essential part of building **inclusive** communities.

ALTHOUGH WE MAY LIVE IN BIG CITIES, AND OUR SMARTPHONES ALLOW US TO TALK TO OTHERS AT ALL TIMES, MANY PEOPLE STILL FEEL DISCONNECTED IN THEIR COMMUNITIES.

VOLUNTEERING IN THE COMMUNITY

Volunteering can help make a neighborhood community a better place to live, work, and play. Volunteers can help look after the areas in which people live, by doing things such as picking up litter, or painting and repairing buildings. Volunteering can also help make everyone feel connected and welcome in a community. Volunteers who visit and assist elderly community members, newcomers, or other people in need help them feel less alone, and more involved in the community. Other volunteers might raise awareness and money for global causes and send help to those who need it. Volunteers can help make all people feel that they are part of a community that cares about them— whether that community is local, national, or even global.

ACTIVISM IN THE COMMUNITY

Activism can help strengthen a community because it starts conversations about our values and what we care about. It can make sure that everyone in a community is treated equally. Activism can get people working together on issues they care about, such as looking after animals or protecting **free speech**. Activism can also show people that they are welcome in a community. For example, a march that supports LGBTQ communities shows that people of all genders and sexual orientations are welcome in that community.

ANONYMITY AND CELEBRITY

If someone has anonymity, it means that their true identity is not known—that person is anonymous. Celebrity is the opposite. It means that a person is known by many. They might be famous. Have you heard of a person making an anonymous donation? How about a celebrity speaking out for a cause? Anonymity and celebrity are related to volunteering and activism in interesting ways.

ANONYMITY

Sometimes, anonymity can be a good thing when it comes to volunteering for a cause. When issues are sensitive, a person seeking help might want to remain anonymous, or ask that the person helping them is anonymous, too. For example, in many countries there are anonymous help lines for children, youth, and adults who are experiencing personal issues. Because the volunteers and the callers can remain anonymous, people can speak openly and receive help without risk of judgment.

THE **SEC** WHISTLEBLOWER PROGRAM IS AN OFFICE IN THE UNITED STATES THAT PROTECTS AND REWARDS WHISTLEBLOWERS WHILE KEEPING THEM ANONYMOUS.

Anonymity is very important for some activists, such as whistleblowers. These are people who release secret information about illegal or unethical behavior by an organization or government. Most whistleblowers need to be anonymous to be able to safely release the information, without repercussions from the organization or government. Sometimes, their identities are revealed after the information is released.

Edward Snowden is a whistleblower who, in 2013, leaked information about how the American government was spying on American citizens. He first remained anonymous, because he knew that the American government would arrest him for leaking the information. He later revealed his identity in a British newspaper. He said that he did this so he could explain to the public exactly what was happening.

SNOWDEN CURRENTLY LIVES IN A SECRET LOCATION.

ANONYMOUS

Anonymous is the name for a group of Internet activists. They are known as "hacktivists" because they **hack** into the websites of governments and organizations all over the world. They sometimes do so to expose issues or wrongdoing. Their anonymity is powerful because nobody knows exactly how many members they have and what they can do. They are able to carry out activism online without being revealed. However, their activities are often illegal.

> TO KEEP THEIR IDENTITIES SECRET, MEMBERS OF ANONYMOUS WEAR MASKS IN PUBLIC AND IN FRONT OF CAMERAS.

CELEBRITY

Celebrities can be famous for all kinds of reasons, and they get a lot of attention from their fans. This means their words have a lot of influence. Celebrities tend not to remain anonymous when giving to charity or being an activist, because they can use their identity to draw a lot of attention to a charity or cause.

EMMA WATSON

Emma Watson is a famous actress and activist. She has traveled all over the world to promote gender equality and women's rights. Watson has helped spread the important message of equality. She is now the **United Nations** (UN) Women **Goodwill Ambassador**. In her role as an ambassador, she led a campaign called #HeForShe, encouraging men to speak up for women's rights. Do any of the celebrities you follow promote causes or engage in activism?

23

INTERNET ACTIVISM

For most of history, communication between people in different places was limited. Before radio, television, and the Internet, it was almost impossible to learn about events happening around the world and get involved in supporting a cause. Today, we have far-reaching forms of communication. A great deal of information and opinions are shared over the Internet. Social media, blogs, and **forums** provide places for people to share information about global issues and to speak out about the causes about which they care.

The Internet allows injustices to be witnessed, recorded, and shared all around the world. It can be an effective tool to help activists be heard. Many people, for example, use the social media platform Twitter to speak out against injustices they experience and observe in the world around them. The Internet can also be used to organize protests. During the **Arab Spring uprisings** between 2010 and 2012, social media was used to gather support—helping to spread revolutions against unethical governments in many Middle Eastern and North African countries.

Imagine a World
Without Free Knowledge

For over a decade, we have spent millions of hours building the largest encyclopedia in human history. Right now, the U.S. Congress is considering legislation that could fatally damage the free and open internet. For 24 hours, to raise awareness, we are blacking out Wikipedia. Learn more.

Make your voice heard

Facebook Google+ Twitter

TO PROTEST, WEBSITES SUCH AS WIKIPEDIA STAGED A "BLACKOUT," IN WHICH THE PAGE ONLY DISPLAYED A MESSAGE ABOUT SOPA AND PIPA.

SOPA AND PIPA

In 2011 and 2012, members of the United States government introduced two **bills** called SOPA and PIPA. The bills would give the government permission to block websites that contained stolen content or that sold counterfeit goods. However, many people were concerned that these bills might lead to websites being shut down unfairly, censoring the content that can be found on the Internet. Companies such as Google, Facebook, and Twitter spoke out, and many activists took part in online protests, and signed petitions. This Internet activism was so effective that the bills did not become law.

SLACKTIVISM

Some people think that Internet activism is not useful. They argue that it is too easy to share or "like" something without knowing the full story. People might spread **misinformation** accidentally. With so much information online, it is also easy to quickly forget about an issue. People argue that sometimes social media activism does not lead to change in the real world. They call this "slacktivism."

KONY 2012

People who argue that "slacktivism" is an issue point to social media movements that did not result in change, such as the Kony 2012 video. In 2012, the video became popular online. It was about Joseph Kony, a Ugandan **rebel** who used child soldiers to fight against the Ugandan government. Many people agreed that it is wrong to send children to fight. They shared the video and some even took part in some protests in their communities. However, finding Kony was a complicated issue. Although many people shared the video, Kony was never caught.

Many people think that the word "slacktivism" is not helpful. They argue that sharing and liking information about global issues is better than doing nothing at all. They point out that liking and sharing information can raise awareness about an issue. It is also a way for people who are unable to participate in other forms of activism to get involved. Despite the fact that it failed to bring about real change, the Kony 2012 video showed a generation of young people that social media can be used for good. Looking at the Kony video can be an important lesson in how social media activism should not end with a "share."

GETTING INFORMED

It is important that people learn as much as they can about a subject before they get involved. There are many ways to learn about global issues. A person could search for and watch documentaries about the subject. They could check their local library for books and search online for news articles. They could listen to **podcasts**, and read online blogs or social media posts to learn about different opinions. It is important to find information from multiple perspectives, to get a full picture of an issue.

THE "BUBBLE"

Do you ever notice that you see the same kinds of articles suggested on your social media again and again? In fact, this is done on purpose. Social media uses **algorithms** that track the posts you like, so that sites can show you similar posts in the future. This means that if you "like" a certain kind of article, you are likely to keep seeing that kind of information. Some people describe this as a "bubble" of information online. The problem with the "bubble" is that you may not be learning information that comes from other perspctives. If someone only reads about viewpoints with which they agree, they may develop a one–sided view of an issue.

IT IS IMPOSSIBLE TO DEVELOP A FULLY INFORMED OPINION ON AN ISSUE WITHOUT HEARING ABOUT IT FROM DIFFERENT PERSPECTIVES.

FINDING A CAUSE

There are many ways to volunteer or be an activist. It can take time to discover a cause or a charity that you want to spend your time supporting. Most people volunteer in a way that suits them, and their skills and interests. If they have a skill that is useful, they may want to use it to help people. Once a person knows the best way to make a difference, they can begin by volunteering or taking part in activism. It is normal to want to make a difference, but to be unsure where to start. Try speaking to trusted adults about your interests. Check if your school or community has volunteer programs. Stay informed about global news and issues and take note if something interests you. There may be a way to get involved!

YOUR SCHOOL MIGHT HAVE A VOLUNTEER PROGRAM THAT MATCHES STUDENTS WITH A CAUSE THEY CARE ABOUT.

PEACEFUL ACTIVISM

Learning about different perspectives can sometimes open up conflict between people who disagree. It is important that an activist or volunteer who cares strongly about an issue can calmly listen to the perspectives of others. It's okay to disagree—but to be an informed activist, a person needs to remain peaceful and treat those who disagree with respect.

GETTING INVOLVED

WEBSITES

To learn about issues and find volunteer opportunities, many people use websites that list organizations for which people can volunteer. They might also check websites in their local communities, which list volunteer opportunities.

In the United States, try websites such as:
www.nationalservice.gov/serve
www.volunteer.gov

In Canada, this website connects citizens with volunteer opportunities:
https://volunteer.ca

Each country and community has different websites with information about volunteering. Volunteers can find the right sites with a quick search on the Internet.

GETTING INVOLVED WITH VOLUNTEERING

If you are thinking about volunteering, check the websites above to find a cause about which you care. If you aren't sure, see if your school organizes any volunteer opportunities. Your teacher may also know of places you can volunteer, and ways that you can help out in your community. You could ask your parents or other community members if they have volunteer experience or know of any ways to get started with volunteering.

ACTIVISTS SPEAK OUT ABOUT ISSUES THAT MATTER TO THEM. ENVIRONMENTAL ACTIVISTS MIGHT SPEAK AGAINST HUMAN ACTIVITIES THAT CONTRIBUTE TO CLIMATE CHANGE. THE FIRST STEP TO ACTIVISM IS ALWAYS RESEARCHING THE ISSUE.

SOCIAL MEDIA AND THE INTERNET

Today, people usually get involved with activism through the Internet. When they have a cause in which they believe, they find like-minded people on social media, or search for websites which can tell them more about the subject. Many activist causes, such as the Black Lives Matter movement, have detailed websites which can tell activists about upcoming events and ways to get involved. Social media can also be a great way to get involved in activism. You could follow activists you admire on social media to get started.

GETTING INVOLVED WITH ACTIVISM

If you want to get involved with activism, ask your parents or teacher for advice. Make sure your parents or guardians know if you are getting involved with activism online. Research and activism on the Internet can be complicated. There is a lot of misinformation online. There are also people who try to gather support for unethical causes. It is important that someone can check that you are getting your information from trusted and accurate sources.

29

THINK ABOUT IT

1 Can you think of examples of volunteering and activism that you have seen in your community? What about examples in your country, or in the global community?

2 Have you been involved in volunteering or activism before? Share your experiences with a peer. How did the experience make you feel?

3 Why is activism important in our world? Use one of the examples in this book to explain the big impact that activism can have in creating positive change.

4 Check out the websites and strategies on pages 28 and 29. Find a cause that is important to you and share it with a peer. How could you get started by making a change in your community?

GLOSSARY

actively Do something in a purposeful, energetic way

algorithms Instructions that tell computers what to do, and how to do things

Arab Spring uprisings Protests and demonstrations held in countries across the Middle East and North Africa, beginning in late 2010, with some lasting until 2012. The pro-democracy protests fought against corrupt governments that kept standards of living low for citizens.

art installations 3-D pieces of art set up in a gallery or outside in public

bills In some countries, bills are proposed laws that need to be passed, or agreed upon, by government

campaigning Putting in organized efforts to achieve a goal or outcome

carbon dioxide A gas found in air that is absorbed by plants during the process of photosynthesis. It is produced when carbon is burned or humans or animals breathe out.

chemical A substance that has been used or produced in a chemical process

child labor Employing children as workers, especially illegally

climate change A change in the usual weather due to Earth's increasing temperature

curriculum The guidelines that instruct teachers which subjects and concepts to teach students

democratic Describes a society in which people vote to elect the people who will represent them in government

discrimination To treat a person or group differently because of characteristics such as race or age

drives Organized efforts, often events or ongoing campaigns, to meet goals or gather support

forums Websites for discussions

free speech The ability to speak freely without fear of punishment

global community All of the people who live on Earth

global warming The gradual warming of Earth's temperature, caused by human activity

Goodwill Ambassador A person who acts as the face of an organization, to spread a message for a cause

government surveillance Watching or observing the activities of a person or group, carried out by a government

graffiti Writing or drawings on walls or other surfaces in public places

hack Use a computer to find secret information

hashtag A word or phrase used on social media and preceded by a "hash" or "pound" symbol

inclusive Equally including all people

Indigenous Refers to the first inhabitants of a place

injustice Unfairness; an undeserved outcome

media coverage The amount of attention, and the portrayal, of something in mass forms of communication including movies, music, and television

misinformation False or inaccurate information

ozone layer A layer in Earth's atmosphere which absorbs much of the Sun's harmful, ultraviolet light, stopping it from reaching Earth

parties Organized groups with similar politicial views who come together to hold government positions

persuading Changing someone's opinion

podcasts A form of audio media, which is recorded and broadcast for an audience

politician A person who is professionally involved in government and politics

power plants A station where electricity is produced

procession A group of people moving in a line

protest Express objection, or an event in which people gather to express objection

racism Wrongly believing that a person's race determines their characteristics, and treating someone with prejudice or discrimination based on their race

rebel A person who acts in opposition to government

refugees People forced to flee their homes during conflict

SEC Short for the U.S. Securities and Exchange Commission, a government agency that protects investors and markets

segregation Separating groups of people; in the U.S., black and white people were legally segregated by race from 1877 to the 1950s

sit-in A protest in which a group stays in a place and, usually, does not leave until demands are met

substances A type of matter with certain properties

unethical Morally wrong

United Nations An international organization of 193 countries, meant to encourage world peace and work to solve global issues

walkout A protest in which a group walks out of a place in which they have responsibilities or obligations

INDEX